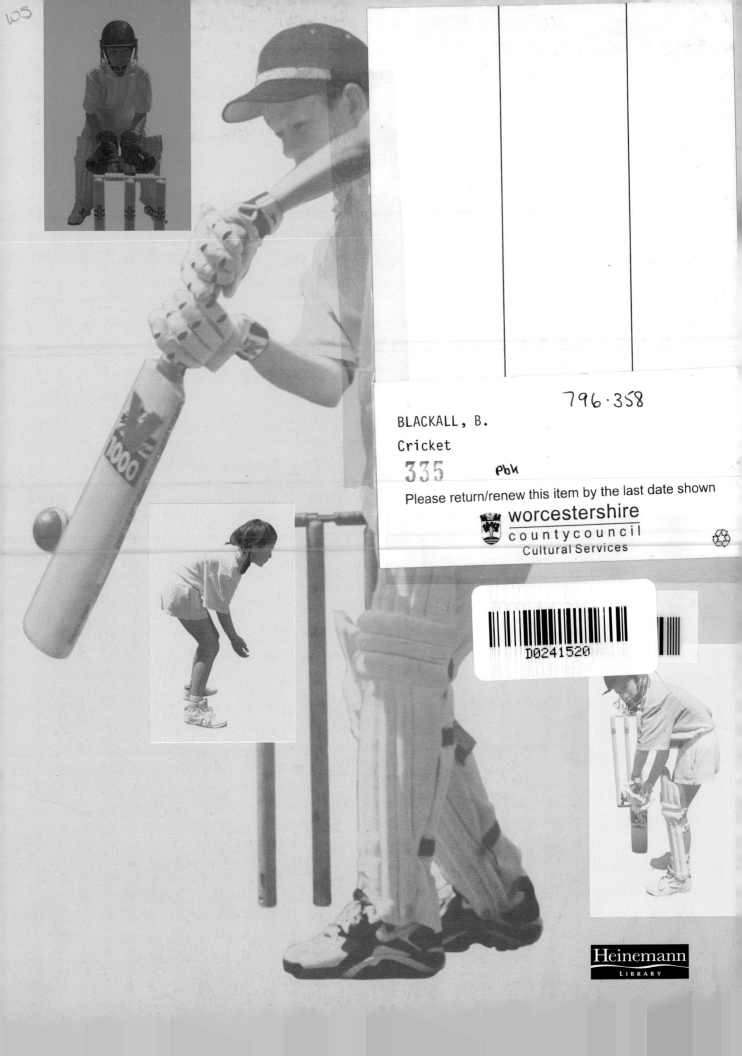

First published in Great Britain by Heinemann Library,
Halley Court, Jordan Hill, Oxford OX2 8EJ,
a division of Reed Educational & Professional Publishing Ltd.

02 01 00 99 98
10 9 8 7 6 5 4 3 2 1

Series cover and text design by Karen Young
Paged by Jo Pritchard
Cover by Smarty-pants Design
Edited by Jane Pearson
Cover photographs by Malcolm Cross and Wies Fajzullin
Illustrations by Joy Antonie
Production by Alexandra Tannock
Printed in Hong Kong by Wing King Tong

ISBN 0431 08505 6

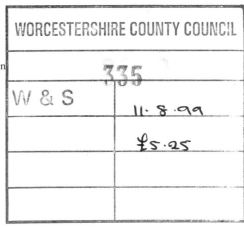

British Library
Cataloguing in Publication data:

Blackall, Bernie.
   Cricket. - (Top Sport)
   1. Cricket – Juvenile literature.
   I. Title
   796.3'58

This title also available in hardback edition ISBN 0431 08500 5.

Acknowledgements
The publisher would like to thank Rebel Sport, Prahran; students from
Armadale Primary School – Robert Klein, Nicola Murdock, Khoa
Nguyen, Mimosa Rizzo, Andrew Scott, Charlotte Scheck-Shaw, Zheng
Yu; Malerie Weston and Debbie Wall for their help with this book.

Special thanks to Peter Burke, nationally accredited level 3 coach,
lecturer Deakin University, Australia and to Chris Oxlade.

Photographs supplied by:
Malcolm Cross, pages 4, 17, 18, 19, 25, 26, 27, 28, 29; Wies Fajzullin,
pages 10, 13, 17; National Library of Australia, pages 8, 9; Women's
Cricket Australia, pages 5, 13, 16, 21, 24; Empics pages 6, 7.

Contents

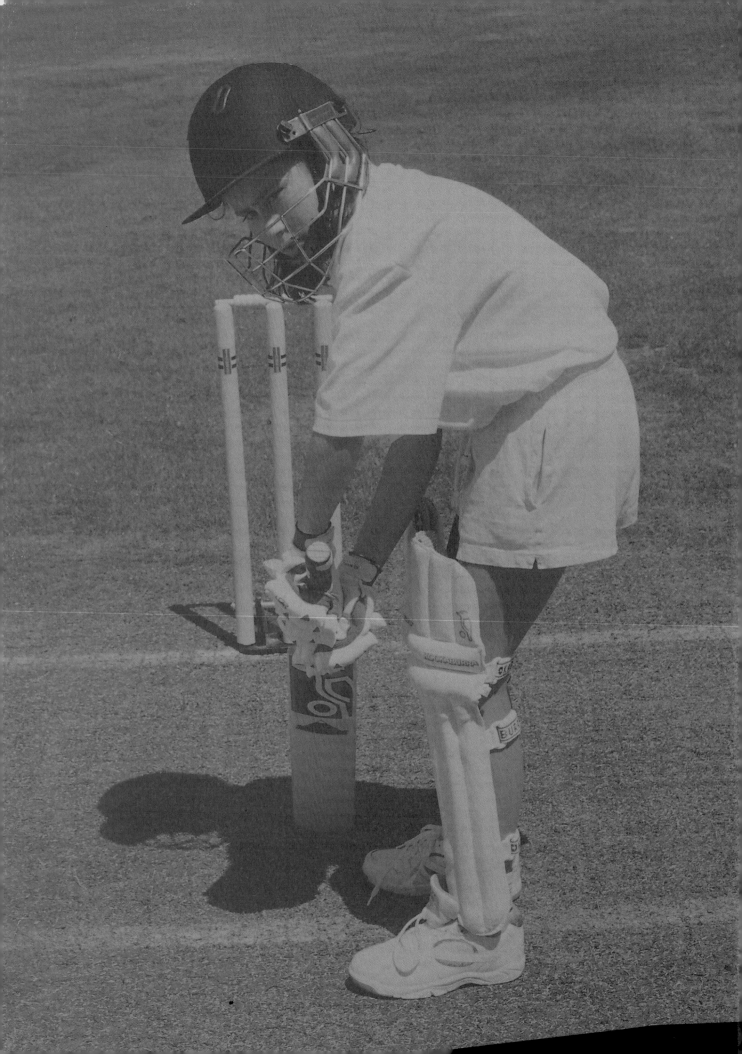

About cricket

Cricket is a bat and ball game played by two teams of 11 players. One team bats while the other fields. This is called an **innings**. The object of the batting team is to score runs. The fielding team tries to **dismiss** the batters (get the batters out), and to stop them from making runs. When 10 batters are out, the fielding team goes in to bat for its innings. The team that scores the most runs at the end of a complete match is the winner.

A coin is tossed to decide which team will bat first. The batting team sends in its first two batters. They stand at either end of the **pitch**. The first batter faces the bowler at the **striker's end**, ready for the first ball. The second batter stands at the other end waiting for the opportunity to run.

The captain of the fielding team places the players on the field. The positions depend on the type of bowler (fast or spin), the type of batter (right- or left-handed), and the fielding team's tactics.

When the fielders are in position and the batters are ready, play starts. The bowler bowls the first ball of his **over** of six balls up the pitch to the batter at the striker's end. The batter tries to hit the ball and make a run.

There are two kinds of cricket match. First class cricket, including Test matches, involves two innings for each team and is played over four or five days. Each innings lasts until 10 batters are out. One-day matches are played in one day and involve one innings for each team. Each innings contains a limited number of overs, regardless of how many batters are out.

UK highlights

Lord's and the MCC

Lord's cricket ground in north London is the headquarters of cricket. It is also the home of the Marylebone Cricket Club or MCC, which was founded in 1787. The MCC controlled English and international cricket until 1968.

The English cricket team is made up of players from both England and Wales, who normally play for county sides. Scotland and Ireland (made up of players from Northern Ireland and the Irish Republic), and also Holland, have international teams which also play against the county sides in some of the UK domestic cricket competitions.

County competitions

Each summer, eighteen English and Welsh counties play in a league competition called the County Championship. Games last four days with two innings for each team. There are also three one day competitions — the Sunday League, played in coloured clothing, the NatWest Trophy and the Benson and Hedges Cup.

Mike Atherton

England skipper Mike Atherton is a determined opening batsman who has played many match-winning and match-saving innings for England in the 1990s.

During the 1997 Ashes series in England, Mike Atherton became England's longest-serving Test captain.

Mike Atherton in action against South Africa

Darren Gough

Yorkshire fast bowler Darren Gough is a favourite with the crowds at all of England's test grounds because of his wicket-taking bowling and spirited lower-order batting.

Darren Gough in splendid form takes his fifth wicket in South Africa

History of cricket

The exact origins of cricket are unknown. It probably developed from games where players used sticks to hit stones and lumps of wood.

In the 1600s, cricket was played by peasants and shepherds in England. But by the 1700s, royalty and wealthy people were playing cricket and it became known as a 'gentleman's' game. The official rules of cricket were written in 1788 by the Marylebone Cricket Club in London.

The first 'All-England' team played matches against other sides around England in the 1840s. The English county game began in the 1700s with one-off matches between teams from counties around London. The County Championship began in 1873.

In 1861, the English cricket team toured Australia. Then, in 1868, an Aboriginal team set sail for England, becoming the first Australian team to travel overseas. They played 47 matches against the English, barefoot!

The first Australian cricket team to tour England.

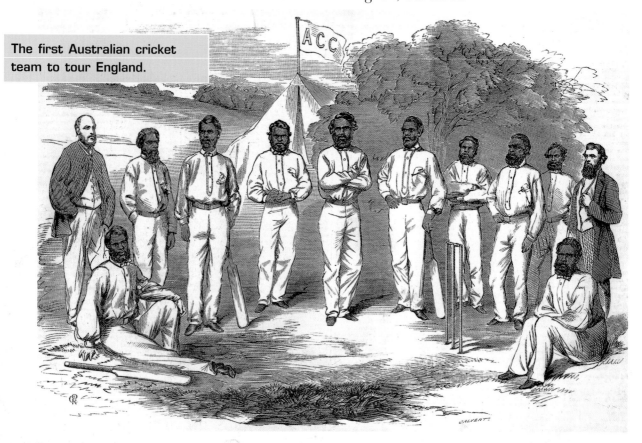

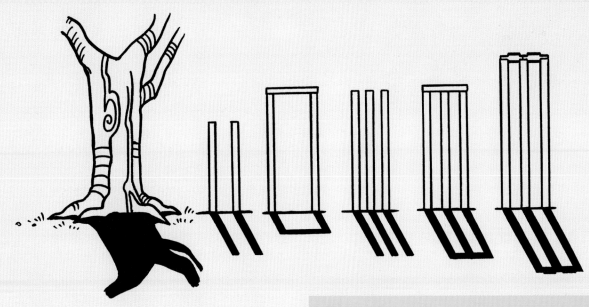

The British took cricket with them as they colonised parts of the world. The first Test match was played in 1877 between England and Australia in Melbourne. New Zealand first competed in Test matches in 1929. One-day international matches began in 1972.

Today first class cricket is played by Australia, New Zealand, England, South Africa, the West Indies, India, Pakistan, Sri Lanka and Zimbabwe. Many other countries including Scotland, Ireland, Bangladesh, Canada, Italy and Holland have teams which play one-day international cricket.

Stumps

Some stories suggest that 'cricket' was first played in forests where trees were used as wickets – this might explain the term 'stumps' as another name for wickets.

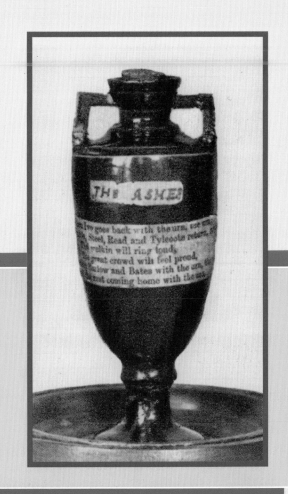

The Ashes

Since 1883, Australia and England have played Test cricket for an urn of ashes! When the Australian team toured England in 1882 and won, local women burned a bail, put the remains in an urn and presented them to the Australian captain. Test matches between Australia and England have been played for the Ashes ever since.

Rules

The field and the pitch

Cricket is played on a grass field. Its size and shape can vary. The **pitch** is in the centre of the field. For first class cricket, the pitch is an area of very hard prepared turf 20 metres from wicket to wicket and three metres wide. A slightly shorter pitch made of concrete covered with matting may be used by younger players. At the edge of the field is the boundary. It can be the fence around the field or a line marked on the ground.

At each end of the pitch is a set of three wooden stumps with two wooden **bails** on the top. The stumps and the bails form a target called the **wicket**.

Two umpires control the match. One watches play from behind the wicket at the bowler's end, the other stands in the field to the side of the batter.

There are lines called creases marked on the pitch. The line on which the stumps are placed is called the bowling crease. There is a **popping crease** (also known as a batting crease) 1.2 metres in front of each bowling crease and **return creases** at either side of the wicket.

Scoring runs

There are three ways of scoring runs:
- Hitting the ball and running between the wickets before the ball is returned by the fielding team
- Hitting the ball to the boundary (for four runs) or over the boundary without bouncing (for six runs)
- Being awarded **extras** from errors made by the fielding team.

Hitting the ball and running

When the striker hits the ball he or she scores one run by running to the popping crease at the bowler's end of the pitch while the other batter runs to the **striker's end**. The batters may run several times before the ball is returned to the wicket. But they don't have to run – if the ball is fielded and returned to the wicket quickly, a batter might be run out.

If a fielder returns the ball wildly to the wicket and it is missed, the batters may continue to run between the wickets. The 'extra' runs, called overthrows, are added to the striker's score.

Hitting boundaries

If the ball is hit to the boundary it counts as four runs – batters do not need to run. If the ball is hit over the boundary without bouncing it counts as six runs.

Scoring extras

Runs known as extras are awarded to the batting team when a bowler makes errors resulting in a **no-ball** or a **wide** (see page 12). If the bowler delivers a bye or leg-bye, the batters may run, adding to the striker's score.

A bye

If a ball passes the batter without making contact and the **wicket-keeper** misses it, the batters can run. This run is called a bye.

A leg-bye

A leg-bye is a run made when a fair ball hits the batter on any part of the body except the gloves or bat. The batter must have tried to hit the ball.

Players must touch the ground behind the line of the popping crease with either a foot or the bat, before turning and running again. A batter is 'safe' while a foot or the bat is on the ground behind the popping crease.

Rules

Bowling

Bowlers bowl six **deliveries** to make up each **over**. After a complete over is bowled, a new bowler comes on and begins the next over from the other end of the pitch.

For each ball to count in an over, it must be a fair delivery.

The bowler's arm must be straight when the ball leaves his or her hand – the ball must not be 'thrown'. When the ball is released, the bowler's back foot must not touch or fall outside the return creases, and some part of the bowler's front foot must be behind or on the line of the popping crease. The ball must be within reasonable reach as it approaches the batter.

If a delivery is illegal an extra run is added to the batting team's score and another ball is bowled in the over. There are several types of illegal balls.

A wide

A wide ball is out of the batter's reach. A wide is called when the ball is too far either side of the batter or too high to be reached.

No-ball

An illegal foot position will result in a no-ball. If the bowler's leading foot is over the popping crease or either foot is touching or outside the return creases, the delivery is a no-ball.

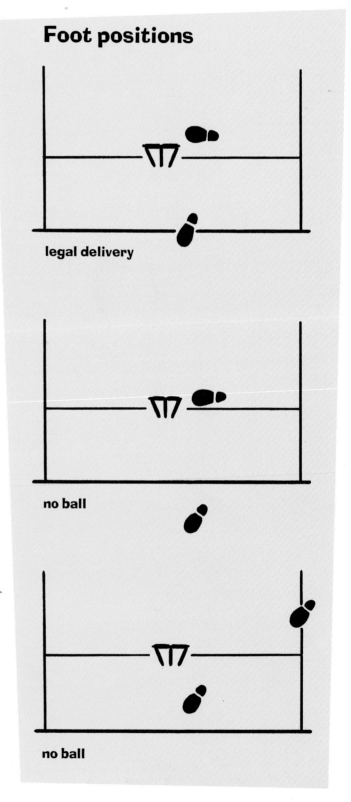

Foot positions

legal delivery

no ball

no ball

Getting the batter out

There are nine ways in which a batter can be given out, or dismissed.

Bowled

The batter is out bowled when a fair delivery hits the wicket, dislodging at least one of the bails from the stumps. The batter is out even if the ball touched his or her bat or body before hitting the wicket.

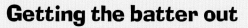

Out bowled

Once the umpire has given a batter out, he or she leaves the crease and walks off the field.

Caught

The batter is out caught when a fielder catches the ball after it is hit or deflected by the bat or gloves and before it touches the ground.

Leg before wicket (l.b.w.)

If the ball is prevented from hitting the wicket by any part of your body you will be out **l.b.w.**, unless you hit the ball first or the ball bounced on the leg side (the side you have your back to) of the line of the stumps.

Rules

Hit Wicket

You will be out hit wicket if you hit the wicket and dislodge the bails with your bat, clothing or body while you are playing a shot. Always be aware of the wicket as you play a stroke.

Stumped

You are out stumped if you are outside the popping crease while the ball is in play and the wicket-keeper hits the wicket with the ball.

Run-out

You can be **run-out** while making runs. If the ball hits the wicket and the bails are dislodged while you are outside the popping crease, you are run-out. Either batter can be run-out regardless of which one hit the ball – if you are running to the wicket that is hit and you have passed your batting partner on the pitch, you will be the one run-out.

Breaking rules

A batter will also be out if he or she breaks any of the following rules:

- A batter must not handle the ball while it is in play.
- A batter must not deliberately obstruct a member of the fielding team from fielding the ball or taking a catch.
- A batter must not hit the ball twice, or stop the ball with his or her body or the bat and then strike it again in an attempt to make runs.

If a no-ball is bowled, a batter can be run-out, but not caught or bowled.

The wicket-keeper has dislodged the bails before the bat has crossed the popping crease. The batter is run-out.

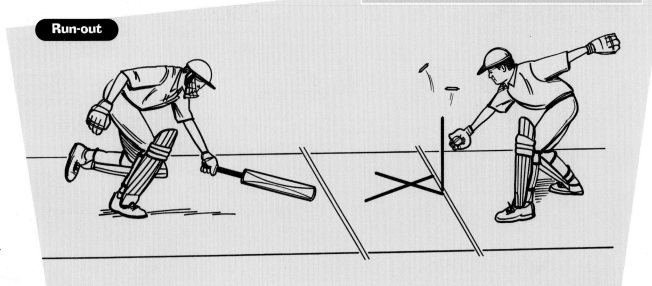

Run-out

The umpires' signals

four

six

wide

out

no ball

bye

leg-bye

What you need to play

You will need two cricket bats, a cricket ball and two sets of stumps for a game of cricket. There is also some very important protective gear that should be used when playing.

The bat

Cricket bats are made of wood. The front, or face, of the bat is flat and straight – this is the part you use to hit the ball.

Cricket bats come in different sizes and weights. When choosing a bat, make sure it suits your height, and that it is not too heavy – a lighter bat will make learning and playing strokes easier.

The ball

The cricket ball is made from cork and twine with a leather covering. The covering is stitched on to the ball and it is this seam that helps bowlers to swing, cut or spin the ball. When the ball is new, it is very shiny. After several overs, or lots of play, it becomes quite rough.

Cricket has traditionally been played in white, but uniforms vary from club to club and according to the kind of cricket match being played.

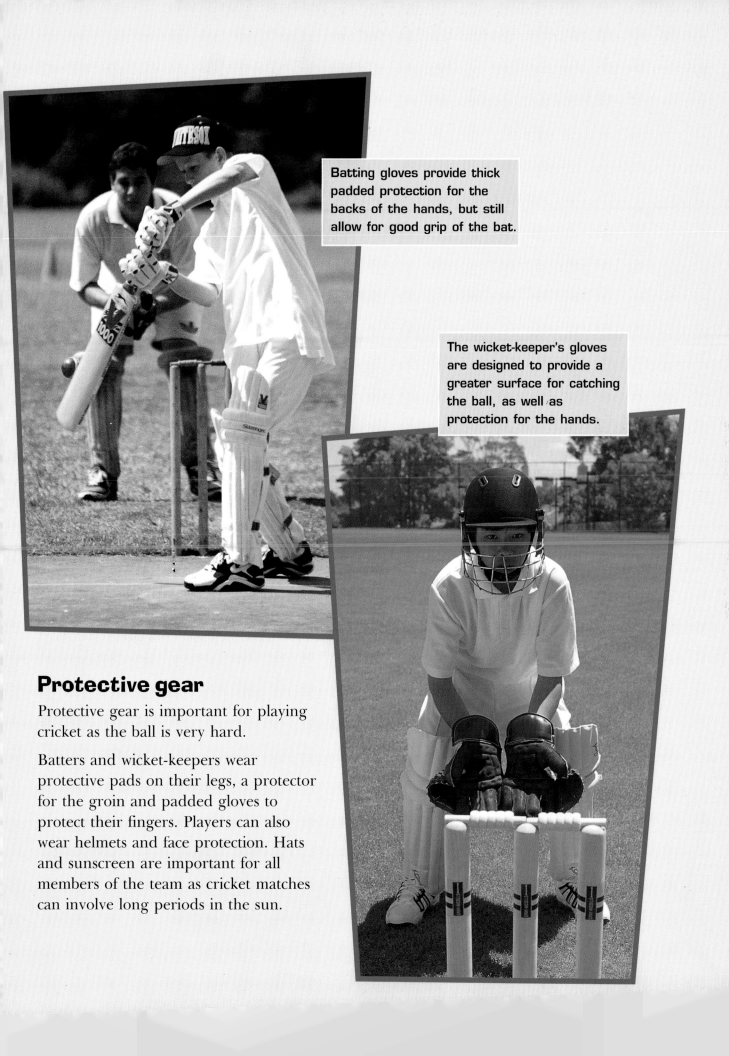

Batting gloves provide thick padded protection for the backs of the hands, but still allow for good grip of the bat.

The wicket-keeper's gloves are designed to provide a greater surface for catching the ball, as well as protection for the hands.

Protective gear

Protective gear is important for playing cricket as the ball is very hard.

Batters and wicket-keepers wear protective pads on their legs, a protector for the groin and padded gloves to protect their fingers. Players can also wear helmets and face protection. Hats and sunscreen are important for all members of the team as cricket matches can involve long periods in the sun.

Skills

To be a good all-rounder in cricket you need sound batting, bowling and fielding skills. You might find that you have more talent in one area and practise your skills to become a specialist batter, bowler or wicket-keeper.

Batting

To bat well you must take up the correct grip and stance.

The stance

Stand in front of the wicket with your feet straddling the popping crease and your weight spread evenly. Grip the bat firmly and hold it so that your hands are just touching your front pad, and the bat rests just behind the toes of your back foot. Watch the bowler very closely. You should be relaxed but ready to play a strong stroke.

The grip

Place the bat face down on the ground. Squat down and pick it up with your hands close together in the middle of the handle. Each hand should form a 'V'. Hold the bat firmly.

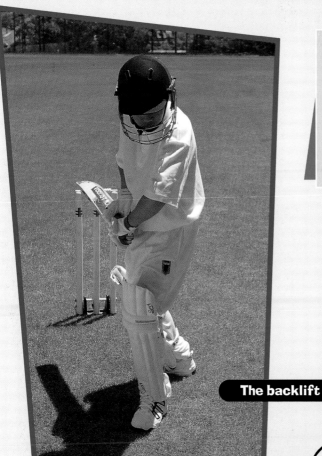

The backlift

Back or forward?

If the ball bounces a long way in front of you, it will be at waist height by the time it reaches you – you should step back to play it. If the ball bounces near you, step forward to play it. If the ball is in between (a good length), decide quickly whether to play it forward or back.

The backlift

For every stroke, you must lift the bat back. Start your backlift as the bowler is about to release the ball. Control the bat with your top hand. Be ready to step forward or back to play the ball, depending on its length.

The forward defensive stroke

This stroke is played when the ball is bowled straight and at good length. Your aim should be to protect your wicket – you are unlikely to score runs from this stroke. Once hit, the ball will bounce just in front of you.

Hold the bat so that it faces slightly downwards. Use your upper hand to control it. Relax your lower hand.

As you lift the bat back, step forward to where the ball will bounce.

Keeping the bat angled downwards, push the ball down into the pitch. No follow through is necessary.

The forward defensive stroke

Skills

The backward defensive stroke

When you are bowled a ball which bounces in line with the stumps and reaches you at just above waist height, play a backward defensive stroke. This stroke will block the ball from hitting the wicket.

The front foot drive

The front foot drive is a powerful stroke, played to a ball that is within easy reach.

Move your back foot closer to the stumps and slide your front foot back for balance. Lift your front elbow high and hold the bat so that it faces forward and slightly downwards – be careful to keep your bat close to your pad so that you leave no gap for the ball to get through to the wicket. Push the ball forwards and into the ground. Do not follow through.

Raise your bat with a straight backlift to about shoulder height. Step out to where you think the ball will bounce. As you start to swing the bat forwards, keep your shoulders and body side-on to the direction you want the ball to travel. Keep your front elbow up and your head and eyes above the ball as you hit it. Follow through in the direction of your stroke and high above your shoulder.

The pull

The pull is played to a short ball that bounces a long way in front of you, giving you plenty of time to 'punish it'. The ball rises to between your waist and shoulder and is bowled either at the stumps or just outside the leg stump (the stump away from the side you are facing).

As your batting skills increase, you can try other strokes to smash the ball through the field to try to hit four or six.

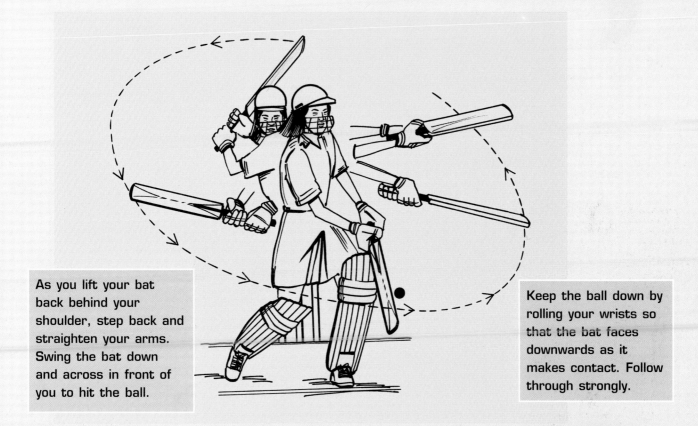

As you lift your bat back behind your shoulder, step back and straighten your arms. Swing the bat down and across in front of you to hit the ball.

Keep the ball down by rolling your wrists so that the bat faces downwards as it makes contact. Follow through strongly.

Running between the wickets

Once the ball has been hit, the batter with the better view of play, usually the striker, will make the call to run or to stay. The most common calls are:
- Yes - if you are going to run
- No - if you are not
- Wait - if you are undecided and want to see just where the ball will go.

Good judgement, accurate calling and good teamwork between batters is essential. A bad call can result in a run-out – you will not be very popular with your team if you get your partner out.

Skills

Bowling

The aim of the bowlers is to deliver balls that will get the batters out or be difficult to play well. It is important for bowlers to vary the style of their deliveries so that the batters are not able to prepare their strokes in advance.

Line and length

Good **line** and **length** are the most important aspects of bowling. The line of the ball is the direction it travels. A ball with good line will hit the wicket. The length refers to the distance along the pitch of the ball's bounce. A ball with good length bounces about 1–1.5 metres in front of the batter. Bowling with good line and length will ensure that the batter is only able to score runs by playing risky shots. If the batter misses, he or she may be out, bowled or l.b.w.

Spin and swing

Bowlers can make the ball spin as it leaves the hand. A spinning ball will change direction as it bounces, making it difficult for the batter to hit. The bowler aims to get the ball past the batter to hit the wicket.

Bowlers can 'swing' the ball so that it travels in a curved path through the air to the batter. Swing is difficult for the batter to judge so he or she is forced to play defensively or risk being bowled out.

Speed of delivery

Fast bowlers aim to bowl the ball as fast and as accurately as possible so that the batter has little time to prepare a good stroke.

The delivery

As you reach the wicket, jump on to your back foot and turn side on as if you are about to do a cartwheel.

The basic grip

The grip will vary for different types of delivery and individual bowlers may make their own adjustments. As a beginner you should start with the grip shown – your first two fingers on either side of the seam. Always hold the ball in your fingers, not the palm of your hand.

The run-up

The run-up adds to the force of the ball as it leaves your hand. Gradually increase your pace as you run towards the wicket. Watch the point on the pitch where you want the ball to bounce. Just as you are about to move into your delivery slow

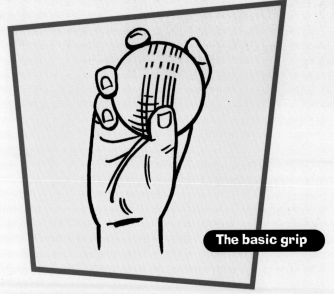

The basic grip

down slightly and jump, turning your body side-on. Land with your back foot parallel to the bowling crease.

Transfer your weight to your front foot. Keep your bowling arm outstretched, head and eyes steady. Reach for the sky with your front arm and thrust your front shoulder powerfully downwards.

Transfer your weight completely to your front foot as your bowling arm comes over and releases the ball.

Skills

The follow through

After releasing the ball, keep running towards the batter for a few steps. This will help you keep your balance and improve the accuracy and speed of your delivery.

As your bowling skills increase, try other kinds of delivery involving variations on the basic grip such as the outswinger and the inswinger.

To complete the bowling action your arm passes down and across your body.

The outswinger

The aim of this delivery is to have the batter edge the ball to the side of the wicket. It can be bowled if the ball has a shiny side and a rough side. Hold the ball so that the seam faces towards the side the batter is facing (off side) and the shiny side faces the batter's leg side. Place your first and second fingers on either side of the seam and your thumb under the ball. Run up and turn as side-on as you can. Release the ball while your arm is high. As you let go, push the seam towards the off side. Keep your wrist firm and straight.

The inswinger

When bowling the inswinger, you are trying to dismiss the batter by hitting the wicket or by striking the batter l.b.w. (leg before wicket). Point the seam of the ball away from the side the batter is facing. Keep your thumb under the ball and place your first and second fingers along the seam. As you release the ball, steer the seam towards the batter's legs. Follow through straight down the pitch.

Fielding

Good fielding is crucial to a team's chance of winning. It helps to dismiss the batting team and it limits their scoring with fast returns to the wicket.

Each delivery the bowler bowls is an opportunity to get the batter out. Fielding requires concentration – the next ball might be the one for a spectacular catch.

Good fielding requires skills in three main areas: catching, gathering and throwing.

The fielding stance

When fielding, you should be ready to move quickly in any direction. Stand relaxed with your weight forward on the balls of your feet. Walk in towards the pitch with the bowler and watch the ball very closely from the time it leaves the bowler's hand.

Catching

Catches win matches! Try to move to a position where your body is underneath the ball. Point your fingers up for catching high balls, and down for catching low balls. Never point your fingers straight at the ball. Watch the ball all the way into your hands, and 'give' with your hands, your arms and your body as you catch it.

You must always be ready to take a catch. Be ready to move in any direction very quickly.

In the outfield, you might get the opportunity to take a high catch. Move quickly so that your body is behind the ball. Stretch your arms up and let your hands give into your chest as you take the ball.

Skills

Gathering

Whenever possible, move to a position behind the ball before you pick it up.

Move quickly to where you will intercept the ball's path. Turn your body side-on with your head, shoulders and arms facing the ball. Bend down on one knee and let the ball roll into your hands. If you miss with your hands, your body will stop the ball.

Throwing

The batters are running while you are fielding the ball, so you must return the ball quickly to the wicket once you have gathered it. Accuracy, however, is just as important as speed. Your throwing action should be side-on, with your non-throwing hand pointing towards your target. Hold the ball in your fingertips and keep your arm nearly straight and your elbow high. Transfer your weight smoothly from your back foot to your front foot as you thrust your throwing arm forward to release the ball.

Lead with your elbow as you propel the ball, and flick with your fingers as you release it.

Wicket-keeping

It is the wicket-keeper's job to catch any ball that the batter misses and to receive throws from the fielders while the batters are running. The **wicket-keeper** takes part in more action than any other fielder.

Take up a ready position. When wicket-keeping to a fast bowler you should stand back from the wicket so that you have time to gather the ball as it stops rising. When wicket-keeping to a spin bowler you should be close enough to reach the stumps in one movement. This is because the batter may move forward to play a stroke and miss the ball. If you are close enough and quick enough you may be able to hit the wicket while he or she is out of the popping crease – batter out stumped!

As the ball leaves the bowler's hand, spring quickly into position to be behind the approaching ball. Watch the ball very closely. If the ball goes past the batter, take it in your gloves, letting your hands and arms 'give'. You might be able to use your pads to 'smother' a difficult ball down to your feet. Keep your legs together and your knees bent.

Be ready to 'dive' quickly to either side to catch the ball. If the batter nicks the ball with the bat, it may be deflected slightly. You might have the opportunity to get the batter out caught.

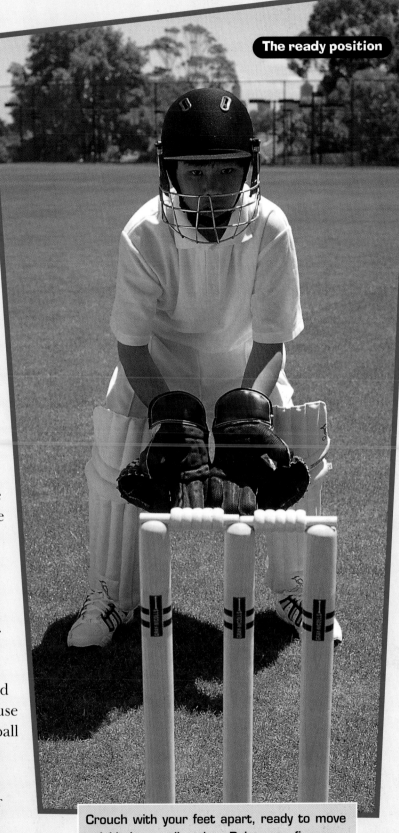

The ready position

Crouch with your feet apart, ready to move quickly in any direction. Point your fingers up or down and sometimes to the side, but never at the ball.

Getting ready

To avoid injury and to perform at your best, warm up with these activities before training or playing. Loose and supple muscles are much less likely to be strained.

Sit ups
Lie on your back with your knees bent and hands behind your head. Keep your feet on the ground and sit up. Repeat 10–15 times.

Shoulder Stretch
Bend each arm behind your head and hold for 30 seconds.

Treadmills
Put your hands on the ground, shoulder-width apart and your legs stretched behind you. Bring one foot forward; replace it and then bring the other foot up. Repeat 10-15 times.

Star Jumps
Stand with your feet together and
arms by your side. Jump and land
with your feet apart and arms
outstretched. Jump back to the start
position. Repeat about 15 times.

Arm circles
Stretch your arms up above
your head and then take
them around in circles. Keep
your body upright. Make 10
forward circles and then 10
backward circles.

Push ups
Lie face down with your
hands below your shoulders
and your toes gripping the
floor. Keep your body
straight and push up with
your arms. (You can also do
push ups from your knees).

Leg stretches
Keep your arms out and your shoulders flat.
Stretch each leg, one at a time, across your
body. Hold the position for a few seconds, then
bring the leg back.

Taking it further

Organizations

England and Wales Cricket Board
Lord's Ground
London NW8 8QZ
☎ 0171 286 4405

(Responsible for all professional and
amateur cricket in England and Wales.
Also contact them for the address of your
county cricket association, which can give
you details of cricket clubs in your area.)

The Marylebone Cricket Club (MCC)
Lord's Ground
London NW8 8QN
☎ 0171 289 1611

Scottish Cricket Union
Caledonia House
South Gyle
Edinburgh
EH12 9DQ

Irish Cricket Union
45 Foxrock Park
Foxrock
Dublin 18

European Cricket Council
c/o MCC (see address opposite)

International Cricket Council
The Clock Tower
Lord's Cricket Ground
London NW8 8QN
☎ 0171 266 1818

Women's Cricket Association
Warwickshire County Cricket Ground
Edgbaston Road
Birmingham B5 7QX
☎ 0121 440 0567

Further reading

Keely, N. *Successful Sports – Cricket*, Heinemann, Oxford 1995
Lloyd, G and Jefferis, D. *Sports Skills – Cricket*, Wayland, East Sussex 1995
Perchard, P. *World of Sport – Cricket*, Wayland, East Sussex 1988
Middlebrook, R. *Take up Cricket*, Springfield Books Ltd, Yorkshire, 1989

Glossary

bails two small pieces of wood which sit on top of the stumps.

bowling crease white line marked at either end of the pitch in the line of the stumps.

bye a run scored from a ball that passes the wicket without touching the batter or being hit.

delivery a ball bowled to the batter.

dismiss to get a batter out.

extras runs added to the batting team's score that result from byes, leg byes, wides or no-balls.

innings cricket matches are divided into innings. Each team's turn to bat is its innings.

l.b.w. (leg before wicket) a dismissal from a ball that hits the batter but would otherwise have hit the wicket.

leg bye a run scored from a ball that is deflected by some part of the batter's body (but not the hands).

length the distance along the pitch from the bowler to where a delivery bounces.

line the direction a bowled ball travels in. A ball with good line will hit the wicket if the batter misses it.

no-ball an illegal bowling delivery because the ball was thrown or the bowler stepped outside the crease. A no-ball results in a run being added to the batting team's score and another ball being bowled in that over.

over six deliveries bowled from one end of the pitch by the same bowler.

pitch the area of hard ground between the wickets.

popping creases white lines marked across the pitch in front of each wicket.

return creases white lines marking the sides of the pitch, within which the bowler must bowl.

run-out if a fielder knocks the bails off the stumps with the ball, before a running batter makes it back to the popping crease, the batter is run-out.

striker's end the end of the pitch that the bowler bowls to. The striker's end changes after each over.

wicket the target that the bowler aims to hit to bowl a batter out. The wicket consists of three wooden stumps with two wooden bails sitting on top.

wide a ball delivered beyond the batter's reach.

Index